Songs Are A Place We Go

A 30-Day Devotional Experience For Worship Musicians

Dan Wilt

www.DanWilt.com

[cover photo credit: Priscilla Du Preez via www.Unsplash.com]

DEDICATION

This book is dedicated to all who lead worship, serve in a worship ministry, or support the formational experience of worship in your local church.

What you do, and *how* you do it, has always mattered.

And it always will.

Let's continue to do this together – for our people, for our time, for the Kingdom, and the King who is leading us Home.

TABLE OF CONTENTS

INTRODUCTION | SONGS ARE A PLACE WE GO

I waited patiently for the Lord; he turned to me and heard my cry. He lifted me out of the slimy pit, out of the mud and mire; he set my feet on a rock and gave me a firm place to stand. He put a new song in my mouth, a hymn of praise to our God. Many will see and fear the Lord and put their trust in him.

Psalm 40:1-3 (NIV)

A number of years ago, one of my cousins went through an unimaginable experience. While working as a humanitarian aid and development worker in northern Kenya, a small band of terrorists broke into his hotel room. He was kidnapped (with two colleagues) and taken into Somalia, where he was held captive in the desert for over two months.

To this day, the stories he tells from that harrowing time in his life remain difficult to hear. I can only imagine the long days and nights passing ever so slowly, with deathly fears pressing in on every side whispering to you that your life will end that day.

(Prayer, in such circumstances, must be quite different than it is when things are going relatively well - and we just need more money in our bank account for that upgrade to our summer vacation.)

With the Holy Spirit working in and through a series of choices he and his companions made, an eventual turning began to occur in the hearts of his captors.

After what seemed to be another lifetime, he and his fellow hostages were miraculously released.

At a family gathering in Pennsylvania following his homecoming, he and I wandered off to a corner where we could really talk.

What Role Did The Music Of Worship Play?

As we shared words of gratefulness for his freedom, I paused to ask a simple question:

What role did music, and worship music in particular, play in bringing him any peace in the midst of this life-altering trauma?

He was quiet for a moment. Knowing my life's work as a worship leader and songwriter, he began to communicate just how important *songs* had been – particularly *songs of worship* – in maintaining his sanity as his well-being was threatened daily.

Surrounded by weapons of death (and people not afraid to use them), he told me how he would sing songs of worship in his head – over and over and over again. And though the heavens did not open to offer him rescue, he was somehow encouraged by the lyrics and spirit of each worship song, moving through his heart from his memory, cutting though those dark moments in his life to offer passing glimpses of hope, faith, and confidence in God to do His part.

In each of those moments, a song became so much more than a weaving of melody and poetic lyrics. Each song became a haven, a stopping place, an encountering ground, for his struggling heart.

Sitting there listening to him, it was clear to me that his story of trust, forgiveness, hope, courage, and faith were fueled, at least in part, by each one of those songs he called to mind.

As he continued to share, I found myself considering the power of worship in the life of a local church.

I found myself becoming grateful for the new songs that God puts in the mouth of the Church, gifts to every generation that widen the beautiful worship work of the Body of Christ moving through time.

I became grateful for the ancient songwriters who offered their gifts in service to the Church, today's songwriters who write the songs that we need to sing, the worship leaders who choose the songs that will matter to us each week, the worship musicians who play the songs after preparation and practice, and the worship techs who make sure the congregation can connect with those songs of life in every way possible, sonically and visually.

That's when a very simple phrase leapt to my mind, with the fragrance of revelation all around it.

"Songs are a place we go."

When A Song Is More Than A Song

Songs are a place we *go*. In other words, a song can be *more* than a song.

A song can be a *place* where the truest and fullest of relationships is nurtured, though without a geographical location (what we typically assign to a place) to hold it down or limit its reach.

A song was the worship liturgy my cousin needed in his most dire moments. A song is a portable liturgy, an access point, that opens our hearts to God.

When you or I lead worship with a song, no matter our role in that worship ministry process, we are guiding ourselves and others to a place of divine-human encounter. Can you think of a higher calling?

Name Your Songs

If I asked you to name 2-3 songs, particularly worship songs or hymns, that have become spiritual anchors for you over your lifetime of following Christ, what would they be? Take a moment to recall them each to mind.

Now, pick one of them, your *favorite*, and begin to hum the tune. Now that you've got the song in your mind, begin to sing the song out loud for at least one or two minutes.

Do you find yourself beginning to *go* somewhere?

Now, can you imagine yourself singing that song at the top of your lungs in your car, in a field, or in your home? There is nothing unnatural about imagining that, is there? It's what we do when we love a song, and a song seems to love us in return.

The song carries you, lifts you, and escorts you to a place of faith and thought that matters to you in your life's journey. In fact, that song will always matter to you.

(If you are young, trust me; the songs you love now will have heat on them for the rest of your days. They will always be a place you can go to meet with God.)

Salvation Singing

Can you recall a moment when those lyrics kept your faith centered and alive during a season when you heart felt heavy, weak, and in need of rescue?

If you're anything like me, those songs spring to mind quite quickly, and each is a *salvation song*. Each song, led by the Saving Spirit of Jesus, has Gospel power that incisively and powerfully cuts through the 31 flavors of emotion we may feel on any given day, bringing a sense of *hope* to our weary soul.

That song, again, will become precious to you over a lifetime. In my moments of deepest despair, I have always found that God gives me a song to sing. It may be an old song, or it may be a new song. The song gets stuck in my mind, looping over and over again in my heart, through dark nights of the soul and bright days of hope.

If I pause and allow myself to consider the song's gift long enough, my heart will begin to hope again.

If you begin to think through your own extended spiritual journey related to songs, particularly worship songs, you'll begin to be able to identify songs that have

- opened the door to a revelation from God,
- softened your mind and heart to receive a fresh insight from the Holy Spirit, or
- literally carried you through an intense season of challenge in your life.

Songs that you call *your own* may be songs that everyone loves, or that few others like. But when the music plays, those songs transport you to another space – a "place" created by the sound, groove, melody, and/or lyrics of that unique work of art.

And the "place" of a song sung in worship, from one whose heart is offering it in "spirit and in truth" to our Creator, is often inhabited by the Holy Spirit.

When a song becomes a place for you, and that place is inhabited by the Holy Spirit each time you go to it, then you have truly found one of God's intimate gifts to you for this lifetime.

A Sonic Sanctuary For Every Christian

Of course, a worship song is just one liturgical tool of the historic, worshipping Church – but it is an important tool that has been used by the Spirit to comfort the saints, to fasten our faith to Jesus, to renew the weary heart, and to put a new song in the mouth of the child of God needing to *sing*.

Whether we are singing an ancient Psalm, the Scriptures, a hymn, an anthem, or a melody and lyric we first heard in a local church, on a YouTube channel, via a music app, or in a worship rehearsal –

songs of worship *matter* to us.

My wife's grandmother was hard of hearing and could barely see. Confined to her wheelchair, we would bring her back to her longtime home in the hills of North Carolina for family gatherings.

She would sit quietly while five or ten conversations bustled on around her. Then, I would bring out my guitar. I'd sit close to her, so she could see my face and hear my voice. I would begin to sing one of her favorite songs of faith, and everyone knew what was about to happen.

Even though the theology behind it is imperfect at best, that song was a place she would go to meet with God.

Some glad mornin' when this life is over
I'll fly away
To a home on God's celestial shore
I'll fly away

I'll fly away, oh, glory
I'll fly away
When I die, Hallelujah, by and by
I'll fly away

Grandma's toes would begin to tap, and she would lift her voice as best as she could. It was a delight to watch, and, even more delightful, to participate in worship with her.

Grandma did go on to God's celestial shore, where today I believe she is enfolded in the Father's loving arms. That song, at least for her, kept her going in faith through many toils and snares along the way.

This is the gift of music, and this is the very special gift of *worship* music.

In other words, a faith song can be a *sonic sanctuary* for a divine-human meeting. A song can be an encountering ground – a portable liturgy for the car, home, or workplace – for those who embrace what only the Spirit can do through a song.

What You Do Every Week

I've spent much of my life encouraging worship leaders, musicians, and technical people, in many streams of the Church, related to their unique roles in local church life.

In particular, I've worked for 30 years now to convince each person who serves in a worship ministry that the special part we play in the lives of our local congregation is invaluable to each person's walk of faith – to each person coming alive, staying alive, and feeling alive in faith, hope, and love.

The road is long, for all of us. A good Travel Song can keep us moving toward our destination to the heart of God. In seminars and conferences, I've often asked the following questions:

If songs are powerful and formative tools of encounter, learning, and spiritual sustenance, then who will lead people, in our generation and each week in our local church, in songs that reclaim for them the great narrative of God (Robert E. Webber)?

Who will lead us in songs that reorient them to the purpose of their lives, to hope, to faith, and to walking with Jesus through the celebrations and storms of life?

Who will lead us in songs that tell the Story of God over and over and over and over until we get that covenant narrative deep in our bones?

Who will lead us in songs that the Spirit uses, along with all aspects of living worship, to conform us and our desires to the very desires of Christ (James K.A. Smith)?

Will Wall Street do it? The world's wealthiest people? The celebrities of our time?

No. They won't. They're busy. They have other values and priorities.

But you and I will.

You and I will feed the Church her sustaining songs of faith, hope, and love.

If we don't do it, who will?

And if you do choose to be a part of leading worship by participating in your local worship ministry, why would you not see it as the incredible blessing it is to those whose life may depend on a song that you sing on a simple Sunday like any other?

You Lead Us In The Songs That Shape Our Lives

When the pain hits and the rubber meets the road week after week, it is the worship community in a local church that will work with the Spirit to put a song in a person's heart.

We will practice the song that week. We will rehearse it for a few hours as a band. We will set up the lyrics, ride the sound board, and pray the opening prayer that welcomes everyone into worship. *We* will step forward into the ministry of worship.

Why? Because that's what we have been called to do, for a season or for a lifetime.

Songs are a place we go.

You lead us to those places, by the Grace of God, every time you play or do your part.

About This Devotional

This 30-day devotional experience is dedicated to you as a worship ministry team member.

Whether you lead worship, play bass, sing, drum, play keys or guitar, set up communion, write songs, do sound, or make sure the lyrics appear in perfect timing to support the congregation as they worship – the words on the following pages are for you.

This devotional is divided into two sections, with 15 devotionals each:

Section 1: The Worship We Lead
Days 1-15

Section 2: The Heart Of The Worship Servant
Days 16-30

In Section 1, we take the first 15 days to reflect directly and deeply on the topic of worship. Each devotional will have something to say about the vast and often mysterious topic of worship.

In Section 2, we take the next 15 days to pause to look at our own hearts and the cultivation of the kind of inner life that can handle a leadership role, a stage, and a purpose bigger than us.

I've also provided some room for your own "Reflections & Notes" at the back of the book, so you can document what moves you.

I've intentionally written these devotionals over the course of many years, for those on my email list at **DanWilt.com**, so I could capture some of my own life and worship leadership experience in each one.

Each daily devotional represents one big idea I believe is important for every worship team member to have simmering in her/his head and heart.

My intent is that if you are a worship musician and/or team member, you would have your own copy of this little book, to refer to again and again over the course of your ministry participation and lifetime.

Each devotional takes less than 3 minutes to read out loud, so the book has a dual purpose: it can either be read personally for your own spiritual enrichment, or it can used in rehearsals and settings where worship teams are gathered, preparing to serve in worship.

No matter how you use this devotional, may it strengthen you in your high calling in Christ Jesus (Philippians 3:14).

Know that I am praying for you and your worship community as you use this book in private and public to orient you, again and again, to the worship ideas that keep our lives and ministries focused on Jesus and His purposes for humanity.

Songs, my friend, are a place we go. Let's lead those songs of living worship, faithfully, for ourselves and for those we serve.

Dan +

Dan Wilt
Nashville, TN

THE WORSHIP WE LEAD

1. GOD SENT A MUSICIAN

David said to the Philistine, "...All those gathered here will know that it is not by sword or spear that the Lord saves; for the battle is the Lord's...."
1 Samuel 17:45a, 47 (NIV)

When a giant needed to be dealt with, God sent a *musician.*

David, the young shepherd who faced down the great giant Goliath, was a musician. While tending to his father's flocks in his lonely life as a shepherd, he had not only learned how to sling stones at lions and bears; he learned how to face down the foes in his own heart through the singing of a song.

People have faced giants, on many battle lines, across history. And whether the giant is personal or cultural, music has played a powerful role in enabling small heroes to take down big enemies.

Believers for thousands of years have found strength singing new songs, creating and experiencing powerful music, and worshipping with courageous melodies that have entrenched psalms, hymns, and spiritual songs deep into fearful hearts.

The torchlight of songs in the hearts of millions brought life, hope, and strength to those facing giants through dark nights of the soul in the American civil rights movement.

Musicians led the singing and writing of hymns that gave Wilberforce and others the bright light of encouragement they needed when the storm clouds were gathering against their work to end the slave trade in England.

Every week, we practice, shape sets, and faithfully lead worship so that even one person in our congregation can feel strength surge in their bones as they declare the goodness, nearness, and favor of God in song.

God sends musicians to help people face their giants *every week*.

And the music, sound, and visuals that support those songs deliver anthems into peoples' hearts that they will need for their battle lines. Songs are as sure to turn the tide in a battle as the five smooth stones David pulled from the stream.

Every giant in the room on a Sunday morning has been served notice – when the people of God begin to sing, fear has met its match.

REFLECTION

How do you see your role in the worship community? How do you see it differently after reading this?

PRAYER

Spirit of God, there is more to what we do when we lead worship than most of us imagine. You take the songs we lead and make them stones in the slings of average people facing giants of the heart, mind, and circumstance. Thank You for the part we get to play in inspiring your people to proclaim Your victory in the face of their foes, and to walk forward in trust on the battle lines of life.

In Jesus' empowering, triumphing Name,

Amen. +

2. WHAT IS WORSHIP?

So here's what I want you to do, God helping you: Take your everyday, ordinary life—your sleeping, eating, going-to-work, and walking-around life—and place it before God as an offering. Embracing what God does for you is the best thing you can do for him.
Romans 12:1 (*The Message*)

Since the beginning of time, people have worshipped. There may be no more primal impulse in human beings - Spirit-born creatures who eat, drink, think, hope, and love - than responding with awe to the sacred world in which we live.

And when we get beyond our awe to perceive the Person behind it all? The door is open for us to worship the One true God, as we were made to do.

So what is worship? While there are many ways to answer that question, a question that is at the heart of thousands of historic books, Romans 12:1 captures its essence in a way that draws on the liberating passion of the Hebrew idea of *covenant*, and the enlivening power of the Gospel.

"Take your everyday, ordinary life... and place it before God as an offering...." Or, to put it another way, *"...Present your bodies as a living sacrifice... which is your spiritual worship."*

Worship is a whole-life response of the believing heart, through all means available, to the Eternal God - the God who has self-revealed in the Trinitarian unity of Father, Son, and Holy Spirit.

It is, drawing on the First Testament image, a covenantal response of *allegiance* - an act of freely given love and intimate friendship evidenced in gratefulness, trust, and hope.

We obey. We pray. We sing. We give. We love. We honor. We dance. We choose. We receive. We raise families. We strengthen friendships. We work jobs. We seek counsel.

And to support all of this worship wrapped up in living and dying and loving and deciding, we speak the Scriptures, sing the Story, and stand with the Spirit's work in worship, with rhythm and regularity, as we steadily feed on Christ through faith until our dying day.

Whatever we do, we do it all to the glory of God.

If worship is covenant-loyalty to the Trinity in a disloyal world, then every time we lead our community in singing our allegiance, remembering God's Story, and meeting with God through all the acts of worship that are a part of our worship life together, we are equipping them for a daily, second-nature response of worship that will become one of the most life-giving habits of their entire life.

REFLECTION

How is worship more than the songs we sing and the liturgies we use? How is your congregation moved forward in their daily acts of worship by what happens in a worship service?

PRAYER

Spirit of God, the innermost place in our hearts was made for worship, and we release ourselves from other loves in this moment to secure our one love on You. You have loved us with an everlasting love, and as we lead others to be formed by You, Your Word, and Your Spirit in worship, let us experience the same love that has drawn millennia of worshippers to Your heart.

In Jesus' worship-evoking, Spirit-filling name,

Amen. +

3. WHO DO WE WORSHIP?

Do you realize where you are? You're in a cosmos star-flung with constellations by God, a world God wakes up each morning and puts to bed each night. God dips water from the ocean and gives the land a drink. God, God-revealed, does all this.
Amos 5:8-9 (*The Message*)

When I was a young boy in Pennsylvania, I used to lay on a small hill near my home at dusk, gazing up into the star fields sprawled out before me. The feeling that overtook my senses on those cool summer nights remains to me, indescribable. As far away as the Orion star-factory felt from the small island home on which I lived, that was exactly how near God felt to me in those youthful moments of mesmerized wonder.

I knew God, on that small green knoll, as intimately as I would ever know Him in my life – though not as maturely or fully as I would come to experience. I was loved, valued, and supremely swallowed up in a love-soaked grandeur that has only ever been equally touched for me by the language of music.

The butterflies, the evergreens, the waterfalls, the stars, and the graceful deer all speak a language of worship that I've wanted to engage in my entire life, and music somehow seems to bridge the divide for many of us who are drawn to that liminal space between described reality and indescribable transcendence.

The One we worship, from the beginning of recorded time, has been the spark within the fire, the rush within the river, and the mist within the cloud, that has compelled worshippers from every tribe and religion to fall on their faces, crying, "Holy." But often that cry has been ascribed to an unknown God, an unnamed God, or a God framed in our image to make sense of the mysterious *numinous* (R. Otto) to the primal mind.

On a night like no other, in a small village nestled in a Middle Eastern landscape, the unknown but many-named God self-revealed to all the stargazers and wonder-seekers of history.

Carried to that moment by thousands of years of covenant-keeping and self-revealing, the Great Adonai of the ancient Jews flashed onto that Bethlehem scene wearing flesh and blood as royal natal garments.

The "Incarnation," the enfleshing of the illimitable God, in Jesus, the Christ, *happened*.

God the Creator (Gen. 1:1), God the King (Ps. 103:19), God the Trinitarian unity (Deut. 6:4), and God the Savior (Matt. 1:21) unveiled His Person, the personality behind the emergence of the creative human, the royal human, the communal human, and the rescued human of all our best stories.

While reflecting on Who we worship will always carry us into the realm of "things too wonderful for us" (Psalm 139:6) and the Word "made flesh" (John 1:14), the God who bursts out of the maze (N.T. Wright) will always say Who He is so that we can - in worship's eternal response - say it, sing it, and express it back to Him in adoring relationship.

Love self-reveals for a shared knowing to continue the glorious communion and unhindered intimacy of mutual awareness and presence between God and the human spirit.

Who do we worship? The God of wonders, both micro and macro, in the interstellar finite and the spiritually infinite places we call home. Worship, and adore, the Lord Jesus - God expressed in the language of humanity.

REFLECTION

How does worship, in your church, help to reveal the Person of God to your congregation? What part do you play in that ongoing revealing?

PRAYER

Spirit of God, it is You who bridges the gap between what we can know and what we can come to know – should we take the worship leap with You. In the process of my discipleship, shed new and increasing light on Who You are. Let my ever-expanding awareness of Your presence lead me to see my Creator, King, Trinity, and Savior as the true focal point for human affection, and for my own.

I worship You, self-revealing God, and will lead others to do the same. Reveal Yourself to me even as I reveal more of myself to You. I will hold nothing back.

In Jesus' captivating, soul-entrancing name,

Amen. +

4. WHY DO WE WORSHIP?

We love because He first loved us.
1 John 4:19 (NIV)

In the beginning, Love makes the first move. The story of this universe that we feel, see, touch, smell, and intuit begins from Love, was built for Love, and is sustained by Love.

Love begins the Story. Then, we come on the scene – spoken into being by Love, and formed by Holy, Caring Hands. And no sooner do we rise from our cosmic nursery with the breath of God in our lungs and the light of God in our eyes – then we assign ourselves to be the Center of the story, the Star of the Story, and even the Start of the Story.

Love births you, births me, from Love, and we start our very first sentences with "I" instead of "We," with "Me" instead of "You." It is the identity crisis that sits at the center of all human suffering – that we don't know who we are, and we look to ourselves to figure it out. The story grows smaller and smaller, and becomes the normalized Way of the Broken, the Path of the Plotless, and the Fight of the Motherless and Fatherless.

But, into this identity crisis, this search for significance, God speaks.

God, in creating you, says, "You are worth everything to me." And if worship is, in its purest form, to ascribe worth to someone or something, God is the first to do it. We are not to be worshipped as the Beginning and the End according to the Scriptures, but we'd better come to believe that the worth ascribed to us by the Divine One is shockingly more substantial than a polite fondness or affection.

We are worth *everything* to God. Jesus is the proof. A parent struggles to convey just how valuable their child is to them, and it's often embarrassing when we try. Words fail us. Only poetry and tears come close.

By design, God first ascribes precious value and worth to you and I, as a parent would a child, and we respond with thanks. Then we, looking into the eyes of God, ascribe value and worth, ultimate value and worth, and say, "I am worth everything to You, and because of this, You are worth everything to me. And because I am worth everything to You, I acknowledge my worth and value. My identity comes to me from You; not from within me to myself."

Why do we worship? It is a *response* to the already all-consuming love of God for us.

As those who have been valued and treasured by God, we receive that love and offer it freely to others, ultimately offering it back to the One who knows us, pursues us, and is the Starter and Finisher of the Story of Love.

REFLECTION

If worship is a response to God's pursuing love, how does the worship you participate in leading each week enhance that response for individuals in your congregation?

PRAYER

Spirit of God, we worship You as a response to Your great love for us. More particularly, I worship You in response to Your great love for me. I am Your treasure. I am Your joy. And I will worship, and lead others in worship, so that we all might find our identity in union with You.

In Jesus' love-enrobing, identity-establishing name,

Amen. +

5. DOES WORSHIP REALLY MATTER?

Fix these words of mine in your hearts and minds; tie them as symbols on your hands and bind them on your foreheads.
Deuteronomy 11:18 (NIV)

It's a normal Sunday. People are moving into the room to take their seats after driving, biking, or walking to that location. They are regulars, or newcomers, or visitors from many places. Women, men, children all begin to put down their coats, phones, purses, and other items they carried in as if to prepare for something to begin.

And *what* will begin? In churches across the world, the ensuing event will look and feel quite different. But all of those gatherings will have one thing in common – people will be reaching out in the hope of meeting with God, hearing from God, and finding help from God.

People will sing, in most cases. People will pray, in most cases. And, if the Gospel is read and the Person of Jesus is lifted up before that congregation – people will remember who He is, and in turn remember who they are, who others are, and what this strange world is all about.

And if you help us sing, if you help us pray, if you help us hear the words of life and the Word of Life, you will be participating in the changing of people – who then change families, change the lives of their neighbors, change the news, and, ultimately, change the world.

Does worship really matter? If people gathering in a place set aside to see their lives as sacred – to see themselves as God's Beloved-Child, God's Image-Bearer, God's Love-Offerer, God's Deep-Forgiver, God's Generous-Giver, and God's Justice-Doer, God's Heart-Made-Clear – doesn't matter, then we all have better things to do with a Sunday morning.

But if that gathering *does* matter, and what we sing, and say, and pray, and hear, and do is centered on Jesus and the New Creation Life He intends to form in you and I by the Holy Spirit, then worship is the most important activity that any woman, man, or child can engage in every week.

So please, when you lead worship, playing whatever part you play in its unfolding drama, hold your head high. And as you hold your head high, humble yourself to be guided by the Holy Spirit in the details of how, when, and what you do to serve worship happening deeply and beautifully in your community. Make this about the community and their God, meeting in a full, deep, long embrace – rather than about anyone or anything else.

That's why they came. And that's why you are here to serve.

REFLECTION

How does understanding the "why" behind people coming to your church shape your role in worship in your congregation?

PRAYER

Spirit of God, we take our place as worshippers alongside, and along with, our community. Help us take our place in supporting Your work of drawing each person to Yourself, and let love rule and reign in this place.

In Jesus' reason-giving, faith-securing name,

Amen. +

6. THESE ARE THE PEOPLE YOU LEAD IN WORSHIP

Now when Jesus saw the crowds....
Matt. 5:1a (NIV)

I remember it like it was yesterday.

A number of years ago, a friend, who is a photographer, showed me a photo he had taken of our congregation during a worship set I had led a previous Sunday morning.

"I thought you'd like to see this shot, Dan," he said, showing me the colorful image. "These are the people you lead in worship each week."

There, in one picture, was a cross-section of our community. Capturing about 30 people in the back two rows of the large gym where we met as a church, most of those in the image were, in some way or another, people whose stories I knew quite well.

Among those in the picture was a truck driver who had come to personality-transforming faith after decades of alcohol addiction, drug use, and hopelessness.

A computer programmer for a local hospital was in the shot, a man who had spoken great encouragement into my life over the course of many years.

A single mom, a local carpenter, a teenage girl, some college students, a few grandparents, families from a variety of ethnic backgrounds, and a few dancing children were in the frame.

As I looked at the photo through blurring eyes, others in our community flashed across my mind.

Friends from a local mentally-handicapped community, and the familiar group of wild-haired, pierced folks that called our church their home, came to mind.

Homeless men and women, who regularly enjoyed the sense of family and community we embodied as a congregation, found their way to that school gym every Sunday (some even walking for miles to arrive in time for worship).

"These are the people you lead in worship" – it's a phrase that still reverberates in my mind every time I step up to a microphone.

I have never forgotten that moment, and, decades later, it still affects the way I posture myself as a worship leader, musician, and ministry leader.

See who God sees this Sunday, gathered right before your eyes. Maybe take a few pictures to keep them in front of you at other times, and to remind you of all the personal histories that are coming to that moment to meet with the God who loves them.

And, in truly seeing your community, lead them with love.

REFLECTION

Who do you see, or think of, when you think of worship's gift in your community?

PRAYER

Jesus, You are the See-er of all. You see not only the heart, but also the history that brings each heart to the moment we are about to share in worship. Give us eyes to see each person as we lead, that we would lead them to You as their source of hope.

In Jesus' seeing, history-shaping name,

Amen. +

7. WORSHIP IS IMPRESSIVE

And we all, who with unveiled faces contemplate the Lord's glory, are being transformed into his image with ever-increasing glory, which comes from the Lord, who is the Spirit.
2 Corinthians 3:18 (NIV)

When many of us think about worship, we think about it as an *expressive* act – an opportunity for us to communicate to God the depth of our love, our affection, our trust, and our pain.

But while worship is indeed expressive, it can't only be that. As James K. A. Smith has suggested, if worship is predominantly an act of self-expression on our part, then worship's highest goal is for our sincerity to be up to snuff. And you and I being "sincere" is not a healthy way for us to perceive all that is happening in the mysterious act of worship.

To frame worship as primarily being about our personal and congregational self-expression is to, quite simply, make it about *us*.

Worship is primarily *impressive* – it is *formative* – more than it is expressive. In other words, worship is intended to form us, shape us, intensely impress us with and indelibly imprint us with the Story of God, the love of God, the hope of God, and the gifts of God to us in the past and in the now.

Jesus is the worship leader. We are the influenced in worship.

In other words, in and through worship the Spirit of Jesus is leading us, forming us into His likeness, opening us to deliver our pain and struggle into His healing presence, and demonstrating to us the nature of the Good News as revealed in the life and person of Christ.

We are to come away from worship re-oriented to the compounding richness of God's New Creation work throughout history and in the current world, with a view to the bright future, while at the same time having had the opportunity to experience the catharsis that can only come from being honest and truthful with the God who listens, who hears, who comforts, and who indwells.

Worship is impressive; see your role as facilitating your community encountering God in worship for their own spiritual formation, for their enlightenment with truth, and for their renewal in hope.

REFLECTION

How would you say the songs and liturgies you are currently using in worship are forming the hearts and minds of those gathered in your worship services?

PRAYER

Spirit of God, as we come to worship once again, we lay down our craving to see expressions of worship be obvious, dramatic, or expressive. We recognize your deep work in every person in the room, and say "yes" to You shaping and forming their desires toward You as the ultimate goal - through the music, words, and worship actions in which we lead.

In Jesus' impressive, indelible Name,

Amen.

8. WORSHIP AND THE IMPOSSIBLE

Jesus looked at them and said, 'With man this is impossible, but not with God; all things are possible with God.'
Mark 10:27 (NIV)

How many people do you know who can do impossible things? When we think of the impossible, we often first think of someone who can bend the rules of nature, or perform a miracle, a sign, or a wonder of some sort (or at least appear to perform one).

Jesus did impossible things, including seemingly bending the laws of nature – or perhaps rather superseding them by engaging with higher laws at work. But, in this passage, the "impossible" being talked about is the change of a human heart.

Jesus bent the laws of *human nature*.

Is someone bending the laws of "human nature" as miraculous as a leper being healed or a broken ankle being restored? In other words, is it just as miraculous that a fearful person could become courageous, an angry person could become tender, or a hateful person could become loving? If you've ever seen it happen, or it's happened in you, you'll know that the answer is a resounding yes – the changing of a human's inner nature is just as miraculous as bread being multiplied for the masses.

One of the gifts of worship in a local church community is that we are participating with the Spirit of God in seeing impossible changes happen in peoples' lives. You may know of stories, especially in your own congregation, where someone who was locked into one pattern of living, over time, was softened by the water of the Word of God and the worship of God's people.

They walked in the door of your community one day as one person, and they walked out another day as someone barely recognizable to their family and friends.

Make no mistake; while worship is not a magic wand, there is power in an environment where we are singing songs dense with what is true, what is right, and what is lovely. And when it is clear that many of us are *meaning* those songs, from the heart, as we sing them? There is power in being in such a room, and many of our neighbors never get to experience what we take to be so normal. Add to this that the Holy Spirit is active in our midst, moving among us, as we worship, to help us to both will and do the desires of God in the world – and we have a recipe for impossible things happening.

If you participate in leading people in worship, you participate in people experiencing the Spirit who makes the impossible possible in their lives and hearts. And, that miracle is worth seeing again and again and again.

REFLECTION

In light of this devotional, what miracles of transformation have you seen in your life or the lives of others? Have any of them happened in a worship setting?

PRAYER

Spirit of God, there are impossible things waiting to happen this week in the lives of people during our times of worship. Help me to serve with humility, facilitating what You are doing through the unique part that I play in worship. I have no need for glory to come my way when so much glory can come Your way as you work out Your will in the lives of those You love.

In Jesus' transforming Name,

Amen. +

9. THE INFERIOR POWERS & THE WORK OF WORSHIP

And having disarmed the powers and authorities, he made a public spectacle of them, triumphing over them by the cross.
Colossians 2:15 (*The Message*)

The great Victorian pastor and poet, George Herbert, once wrote in his poem "To All Angels And Saints" these words: "All worship is prerogative… therefore we dare not from his garland steal, to make a posey (poem) for inferior power."

While the meaning of Herbert's words may not be immediately clear, I'll offer one interpretation: "We get to choose Who we worship… but to steal glory from the all-powerful God to make a worship offering to some inferior power – that would be downright criminal."

Inferior powers are active all around us, and the enemy of our souls is always out to convince us that they hold more power than they actually do. Think about the powers raging all around you right now – political powers, financial powers, celebrity powers, media powers, personal powers, spiritual powers, sin powers – all the powers that grab our attention and call us to submit to their glory. It's a weighty list, and left to ourselves, human beings have been falling for their glittering gold for millennia.

But Colossians chapter 2, verse 5 comes to the rescue of human beings – so easily swayed by our vulnerability to power (remember the central message of *The Lord of the Rings*?). The power-confronting work of Christ on the cross was to *disarm* all the powers that demand our homage, and to even put them on public display to show their powerlessness by exposing them to the confounding power-reversal of the cross!

The Lord of all things met personal power with humility, financial power with poverty, and political power with servanthood. Real power met inferior power with humility, poverty, and servanthood. And in the conflict, the inferior powers lie broken on the ground. There is no contest.

So what does this have to do with worship? We gather from all the worlds where the power-plays are being exerted on us, day in and day out, and we sing the praises of God! We pray! We read the Scriptures! We fellowship as the family of Christ! We remember! We take our place as the lead worshippers of creation!

The Spirit disciples us through our worship, and forms us through our words and prayers, to become a people who won't give our heart-allegiance to any inferior power.

As the spins on and on, worship gives us an opportunity to rise from the anxieties of our time and to walk as those aware of the inferior powers at work to win us – those who call others to worship the Lord our God, and to serve Him only (Luke 4:8).

REFLECTION

How does worship in your community address the power struggles going on in peoples' lives as they gather to worship?

PRAYER

Spirit of God, the times and the season we are in can push us to our limits, and suck us into believing that all the powers around are in ultimate control. But we remember, here before You, they are not. You are in control, and Your purposes will not be thwarted by the work of any inferior power. Help us, Spirit of God, to remind ourselves of this daily through worship.

In Jesus' humble Name,

Amen. +

10. THE MUSIC WE MAKE TOGETHER

Therefore if you have any encouragement from being united with Christ, if any comfort from his love, if any common sharing in the Spirit, if any tenderness and compassion, then make my joy complete by being like-minded, having the same love, being one in spirit and of one mind.
Philippians 2:1-2 (NIV)

A worship team's capacity to make strong music together, and to lead strong worship together, mirrors their capacity to maintain strong relationships together.

The music we make together, and the worship we lead together, compels us to care for the lives we live together. These three components of effective worship leadership are inseparably bound.

Strong community, coupled with strong musicianship and spiritual comradery, alters the sound coming off the stage. Unseen spiritual dynamics come into play that heighten our capacity to both sync together as musicians and to sync together as a worshipping team and community when our relationships have been tended to and curated toward love and friendship.

I've seen this play out hundreds of times in worship teams in many denominations. If there is competition between the vocalists, you can hear it in the music. If there is distress between two people sharing the stage, it changes the tone of worship over time.

When you care for one another relationally, the result is always an upgrade in effectiveness as a leadership group.

And that effectiveness as a leadership group gets communicated through the music, over time, in a congregation.

If just one musician or tech takes this principle to heart, and applies it over a long period of time, the value of relationships can eventually work its way through the whole team.

REFLECTION

How does your team care for one another relationally? How could you enhance how you care for others on your team?

PRAYER

Lord, the privilege of serving together requires the grace to care for one another as You intended. We say yes to Your pursuing Love for us, and welcome You giving us the capacity to pursue one another with the gifts of kindness, gratitude, and thoughtfulness as we lead. Lift the music we play by first lifting the relationships through which we play it.

In Jesus' beautiful Name,

Amen. +

11. YOU'RE GOING TO BE GREAT

The greatest among you will be your servant.
Matthew 23:11 (NIV)

I love getting up with the sun on a Sunday morning to head in to rehearse with the band.

I love gathering my gear, hauling it out to my old will-it-make-it-to-church-again truck, and splashing a hot drink on my hand as I try to balance my in-ear box on the neck of my guitar case while I wrinkle extra chord charts in the other hand (as I react to the pain of the hot drink overspill).

I love not finding enough time to pre-rehearse that week due to a heavy work week so I'm that "sloppy arranger" leader to whom the band says, "Really? You're working on the arrangement of this song *as* we rehearse?"

I love re-setting up sound gear discombobulated from the night before and starting rehearsal 20 minutes late because the youth band forgot to reset the stage in their delight over the pizza they were about to have post-meeting.

Not.

Don't get me wrong. Like you, I love what we get to do, and the fact that we get to do it together. Leading worship is a privilege. But sometimes, if I'm honest, I say that through clenched teeth.

Sometimes, I confess, I just get tired of serving. Especially if I'm not seeing the congregation progressing in their worship, seeing them absolutely ecstatic with the worship experience, or if I don't see any measurable energy in the room as I give every bit of what I practiced hours to give in that moment.

And I don't always get tired because I'm burned out; I get tired because, like all of us, I get tired of doing the same thing over and over with less "buzz" to keep me excited.

But then, my friend Tom walks into the room. Our rehearsal finishes and I step off the stage to talk to him, finding out he has had a hard week. Tensions at work have him on edge, his job is on the line, and he really needs Jesus to encourage his heart as Monday calls to him from tomorrow.

We hug, and that's all we have time for. We're about to start. I rush over to the media booth to correct a lyric glitch I saw projected during rehearsal, and our visual team leader graciously fixes it before we begin.

Then we're off.

The energy of the community worshipping in the room lifts me, and I'm engaged again with a little more focus. Then, I see Tom in the back of the room. His hands are raised, his eyes are shining, and he's believing the promises of Jesus once again.

I glance around at the band. The drummer's groove matters in that moment. The bass lock-in matters in that moment. The vocalist's sensitivity matters in that moment. The sound tech's attentiveness matters in that moment. The song I selected matters in that moment. Everything, and everyone, matters in that moment.

While that morning may never be spoken of again, over the lifetime of our community people will still be eating and drinking at the feast of that simple worship moment for years to come. Whether they know it or not, they were formed by it.

Your service, my service, matters – because our community matters. Because Tom matters. And because we matter. Let's show up – again, today – with our best.

REFLECTION

There is a silent impact that worship has on a congregation over time. How do you see that impact expressed in the life of your church?

PRAYER

Jesus, Servant of all, You took the time to teach us that greatness and serving others are two sides of the same coin. We each want to be great – I want to be great – in Your eyes today. So I lay aside my tiredness, my distractions, and my mood, to lean in to serving our community once again through the worship experience we have the privilege of crafting with You. I'm ready to serve again, and I say thank you for the opportunity to be like You as I do.

In Jesus' serving, others-lifting name,

Amen. +

12. LEAD FROM THE LIGHTNING

Clouds and thick darkness surround him; righteousness and justice are the foundation of his throne. Fire goes before him and consumes his foes on every side. His lightning lights up the world; the earth sees and trembles.
Psalm 97:2-4 (NIV)

We've all seen it in a dark, stormy sky, and no matter how many times it makes an appearance, we are usually filled with some degree of amazement. It's a creative flash never appearing the same way twice, a discharge of potent electrical force. It can crack a tree, strike fire to a building, or simply appear like Grace, as a spectacle for the dazzled eye.

That phenomena is lightning, and lightning is the result of something unseen happening that leads to its appearance. A meteorological phenomena happens when two masses of air, of different densities and temperatures, come crashing into one another.

The result is a sign, a wonder, a physical glimpse of what is going on between invisible atmospheric forces.

In worship, the Spirit of God, distributing God's great love and will for the human heart, is moving through the room. When a human heart opens itself to an encounter, the spirit of a person becomes the second front in the sacred sky.

And what happens when these two fronts meet? A flash and a crack of thunder later, a quiet miracle has occurred – a person has found themselves in communion with Jesus – and transformations can begin that otherwise may have never had their start.

In worship, a heart can yield to the love of God, a mind can see the error in its thinking, a will can choose to bend in a new way, or the quiet ache of a great loss can be transformed into joy and trust.

All that can happen because worship created a unique space, a holy place, for the front of God's Spirit and our own to meet.

Sometimes we see the lightning, and we should take encouragement when we do. Sometimes, we only hear the thunder, and we should be confident that unseen lightning gave it sound. And sometimes, perhaps the sweetest times, the flashes of change going on in people are occurring whether we see them with our own eyes or not.

Worship is a storm front; lead from the lightning.

REFLECTION

Where you currently see the lightning happening in your church? In worship? The children's ministry? Where?

PRAYER

God that lights up the world, we thank You that sometimes we get to see what is happening in the hearts of those we are leading in worship. We take encouragement from those moments You give us. We are also thankful for the unseen transformations going on when people sing their prayers and meet You in a way that only You and they will ever know. Give us eyes to see what You are doing in our community as we lead worship, and let our own hearts be a storm front today as we do.

In Jesus' awesome, sky-lighting Name,

Amen. +

13. A SONG MAKES YOU FEEL A THOUGHT

God is my strength, God is my song, and, yes! God is my salvation.
Exodus 15:2 (*The Message*)

The great lyricist E. Y. Harburg once said, *"Words make you think a thought. Music makes you feel a feeling. A song makes you feel a thought."*

When it comes to the formative power of worship in the life of the Christian, no words ever rang more true. The ability to mature as a disciple of Jesus can often seem to be more dependent on mastering our feelings than corralling our thoughts.

While both virtues are vital, and feed one another, it is usually a feeling – a gut resolve – that becomes the trip wire for the next good or bad decision.

Songs can shift a mood as a melody takes ahold of our minds. The singing of words can reorient us as the music compels us to fill our lungs with air and breathe out the words shaped by very physical actions in our mouths.

Then, by singing a God song, our minds engage with yet-to-be-felt realities as our bodies resonate with the music – and truth has an opportunity to pounce on the lies slinking within.

Songs help us to feel thoughts, and feeling holy thoughts can fill us with fresh strength to live like Jesus. In worship, a heavy heart can walk into a room burdened and fearful, and in a matter of minutes find itself hopeful and full of faith because of the simple power of a song.

Never minimize what happens when we lead people in worship. Inner revolutions are occurring all over the room, and songs are powerful ammunition for the fight.

REFLECTION

What "inner revolutions" have you heard about happening in your congregation recently? Did your gathered worship times, in your view, have anything to do with them?

PRAYER

God of Emotion, we thank You for the feelings that show us the fluctuations of our hearts within. Use us, and the songs we lead, to participate in the changes You are making in the lives of those we lead in worship. Help us to lead the songs in such a way that our community can sing them, breathe them, and feel them at work in their souls.

In Jesus' melodic, moving Name,

Amen. +

14. THE WORSHIP TEAM IS OUT TO LUNCH

By this everyone will know that you are my disciples, if you love one another.
John 13:35 (NIV)

It has been said that we learn more about another person in an hour of play than in a lifetime of work.

As a worship team, our play is sometimes also our work. We work in ministry together, tweaking knobs, singing songs we love, working parts, finding grooves, projecting words, and worshipping with our community.

It's play, but it's ministry, and by the tiredness we feel at the end of a service – we realize that it's good heart work in which we've participated together.

But here's the rub. We don't fully get to know each other in the midst of the task – whether we're arranging the songs or making sure our monitor sends are perfect.

We need to eat lunch together. We need to laugh together. We need to intentionally pursue moments with other individuals on our team to make sure we truly *see* one another for who we are.

Everyone has a story, and a meal or coffee, or a gathering, is a great time for you to ask someone else who they have been, who they are, and who they are becoming.

Then, over years, actively tease out the details of that story whenever you get a chance.

We are all more than our instruments, voices, and knowledge. We are people – people who love Jesus and are aiming to live a higher life.

So may it be said of your worship team that you are all out to lunch.

Let's enjoy the community God has given us together, along with the task that we have come to love.

REFLECTION

Who do you think you might connect with this week, via text, email, or in person, that would be strengthened by your encouragement?

PRAYER

Spirit of God, give us the gift of friendship with one another. As we work together, teach us to play together. And as we listen to one another's stories, give us insight as to how we can help one another to flourish in life, in faith, and in the giving of their gifts.

In Jesus' love-pouring, friend-supporting Name,

Amen. +

15. WORSHIP & SHALOM

On the evening of that first day of the week, when the disciples were together, with the doors locked for fear of the Jewish leaders, Jesus came and stood among them and said, "Peace be with you!"
John 20:19 (NIV)

The world is always in need of a good *change*.

On our good days, and on the good days in the news, it might be harder to see. But then the clock ticks, a few minutes go by, and we experience the world as the incredibly painful, unjust, fearful, and broken place it can be.

The Scriptures point us continually, faithfully, to the world that is yet to come, and the Kingdom that is breaking into the moment to reveal it to us.

That world will be marked by *shalom* – a biblical word for peace that speaks of a well-being that permeates the spirit, society, relationships, and even the physical world.

Shalom is peace that is perfect and permeating all things; it is the very presence of the Prince of Peace.

Worship is, by design, in all its ways and forms, intended to shape us into people who hold God's *shalom* in our hearts, and demonstrate it through our lives.

What we sing, what we say, what we pray, what we *do* in worship – it is all intended to point us toward the world yet to come – when God's perfect rule and reign is established, and the wrongs of the human condition are all righted. God's presence, in His future world, is the true North toward which our lives are to point.

In other words, worship has a purpose, and it's not just to give us another opportunity to express how we feel to God. Worship's purpose is to point us toward the good life (James K.A. Smith), the renewed life, the joy-powered life, the flourishing, growing, and fully human-powered-by-the-Spirit, New Creation, Jesus-Shaped life.

The songs we sing and play are just one part of what can, what *must* happen in worship. And they have a big part to play, every generation of Christians has discovered.

People find God's peace, God's *shalom*, emerging in their hearts when a song catches fire within and they can't help but recall the words.

Sure, we can memorize Scriptures and prayers that help us connect deeply to God's *shalom* – but songs have a way of re-harmonizing us with the Father's plan for humanity and creation that cannot be easily shaken off.

Ever had someone hum a melody that you wish they had not? The song got stuck in your brain, and was on repeat for hours after the encounter?

The gift of worship, and the music of worship, is that it can dig its way deep into our psyche and continue to teach us the ways of God long after we sing it together.

And when we need a song in the night to help us in our struggle? It is often right there, on the tip of our minds, because truth is embedded in a *song*.

Recognize that, as you play and lead in worship, people are learning about who they are, the part they play, and the state of the world. They are learning about who God is, the end goal the world is headed toward, and the nature of Hope.

Keep God's shalom burning in your own heart as you lead in worship, and welcome others, through the songs, to embrace

God's great vision of the world that is on its way.

REFLECTION

Have you ever heard a teaching on God's shalom peace? If so, what did you learn about it, and how do you think it impacts how we worship?

PRAYER

Spirit of God, the *shalom* vision in Your heart is what I want to lead me on in this journey. Place Your radiant peace within me, like a seed in good soil, and water it through worship. Let me become the person of peace You designed me to be as Your follower.

In Jesus' peace-giving, world-changing Name,

Amen. +

THE HEART OF THE WORSHIP SERVANT

16. UNTIL I ENTERED THE SANCTUARY

When I tried to understand all this, it troubled me deeply till I entered the sanctuary of God; then I understood...."
Psalm 73:16-17a (NIV)

As a worship leader and songwriter, I often find myself deeply identifying with the musicians and lyricists mentioned in Scripture. When reading Psalm 73, I find myself identifying with no contributor to Israel's songbook more than Asaph.

Every worship musician should.

Psalm 73 is a lyrical "triptych," if you will. A triptych is a hinged painting of three panels that illuminates, through visual art and storytelling, an altar of encounter in a sacred space.

In the first half of the Psalm – the left panel of the triptych – a pained Asaph gets deeply honest with God. Even the opening words can be heard as coming from a pained heart and an aching mind.

"Surely God is good to Israel, to those who are pure in heart. But as for me, my feet had almost slipped; I had nearly lost my foothold." (Psalm 73:1-2).

Asaph goes on to express what seems to be an unchecked envy for the prosperity of the wicked – their freedom from common human burdens (v. 5) and their never-ending, always confounding, wealth-driven, carefree life (v. 12).

When reading this left panel of the Psalm, the lyrics seem destined to affirm the utter uselessness of devoted living and purity of heart.

We can imagine hot tears rolling down Asaph's cheeks as he writes the words we translate, *"All day long I have been afflicted, and every morning brings new punishments."*

Then, it happens. A single verse that forms the center panel of our triptych, and holds the two halves of the Psalm together, emerges.

"When I tried to understand all this, it troubled me deeply till I entered the sanctuary of God; then I understood..." (v. 16-17).

I end the verse here because all that follows is what is truly understood by Asaph after his sanctuary word.

A moment spent in a space of worship – be it physical or musical or liturgical or prayerful – completely turns Asaph's attitude to one of adoration and praise.

Then, the right pane of our Psalm triptych unfolds and completes the picture that Asaph's opening grief might have left unfinished.

The Spirit of the Lord, moving in and through worship, *can turn mourning into dancing.*

"Surely you place them on slippery ground...," "yet I am always with you; you hold me by my right hand," "you guide me with your counsel," "afterward you will take me into glory," "whom have in heaven but you... and earth has nothing I desire besides you," "my flesh and my heart may fail but God is the strength of my heart and my portion forever," "but as for me, it is good to be near God," "I have made the Sovereign Lord my refuge; I will tell of all your deeds" (excerpts from vv. 18-28).

The moment of worship is the moment of healing, of reorientation, of focus, of clarity, and of intimacy. When your picture begins in grief, find the sanctuary of God that most helps you, renews you, and strengthens you.

Then, the completion of the picture begun in your life can end in a deeper praise than you have ever known before.

REFLECTION

What Psalm ministers most deeply to you? Have you had moments in your life where worship was a hinge point, a turning point, in a time of need?

PRAYER

Spirit of God, my heart has known the grief, the envy, and the hopelessness that marks the first half of Asaph's psalm. My fragile spirit has failed me, and my mind has lingered, many times, on my pain rather than my hope. Today, lead me to the sanctuary of meeting that is ours to share, and lift me, guide me, to the renewed song of hope that You sing over me.

In Jesus' envy-breaking Name,

Amen. +

17. YOUR NEW MOTHER TONGUE

Enter with the password: "Thank you!" Make yourselves at home, talking praise. Thank him. Worship him. For God is sheer beauty, all-generous in love, loyal always and ever.
Psalm 100:4-5 (*The Message*)

The daily gifts of God are many – vibrant, lush, and ever-present symbols of His generosity.

Finding ourselves in the middle of such lavish generosity we can, by practicing regular rhythms of gratefulness, begin to train ourselves to notice the gifts God is continually strewing across the path of our lives with more regularity – and a deeper appreciation.

Gratefulness is a natural antidote to depression according to neuroscience, and a cultivated practice of giving thanks for the smallest gifts pouring toward us daily, like a rolling waterfall, changes the mind in both physical and non-physical ways.

Thankfulness – gratefulness – is a song-of-the-heart you can begin to write for your own use.

Find your tools that train you for thankfulness; fill your car with the music that lifts you, practice a daily examen multiple times a day, keep a journal on your desk – always ready – to be filled with moments of appreciation. Do whatever it takes to become the new, thankful person you want to be.

Then, resolve to change your speech. Let thankfulness become your new mother tongue, your new first language. Step by step, with continued practice, you will learn the virtue of thankfulness. And, your life will begin to change for the better.

REFLECTION

What ways, or tools, do you currently use to nurture gratefulness in your heart? Are there any new tools that you think might take you deeper, or further, on that path?

PRAYER

Spirit of God, my ability to perceive Your constant gifts is limited. At times my eyes, heart, and mind are so heavy with lack, fear, and an ominous sense of Your absence. I am ready to, like an athlete, go into thankfulness training – that I might begin to see You and Your gifts to me everywhere.

In Jesus' gifting, giving Name,

Amen. +

18. I WAITED PATIENTLY FOR THE LORD

I waited and waited and waited for God.
At last he looked; finally he listened.
He lifted me out of the ditch,
pulled me from deep mud.
He stood me up on a solid rock
to make sure I wouldn't slip.
He taught me how to sing the latest God-song,
a praise-song to our God.
More and more people are seeing this:
they enter the mystery,
abandoning themselves to God.
Psalm 40:1-3 (*The Message*)

Learning the soul art of patience is a deep, deep work that takes a lifetime – for all of us. Something within us, from birth, believes we should have the power to trigger action – from others, from God, and even from ourselves – simply by exerting our will (in prayer, in conversation, or in self-talk).

But hard as we try, hard as we wish something into being, (spoiler alert) we simply do not always get what we want. Add to this a few other facts: If we do get what we want, what we want almost never comes when we want it, or in the package we want it in! *Selah.*

Unless we learn to "wait patiently," we are continually mixing the recipe for lifelong disappointment in the face of constant desire-delays.

Patience, according to the Scriptures, is the antidote to continual disappointment. And patience – like hope – is a virtue that is practiced. We practice things we want to master; we practice them until we are so fluid in their rhythms that our new mastery overtakes our primal nature.

Our new pattern, our new second-nature virtue, dominates over our first-nature response – even when a crisis presents itself.

Today, there is probably something you want to happen so badly you can taste it. But despite the fantasies your mind has created, there is a high probability that thing won't happen today. Or perhaps even tomorrow. Or this year. I'm sorry.

Here is where we work the muscle of patience. We can say, "I wait patiently for You, Lord," as did the Psalmist.

We work the Psalm 40 muscle even more rigorously when we say, "I know that You know my desires, and I know You've done great things for me in the past. Therefore I entrust what I want to You today, knowing that You keep those desires in Your heart, reform them, and set them in motion in Your timing for Your best plan to unfold."

If you are struggling to have patience, then I suggest you find (or create) a favorite musical version of Psalm 40 and sing it. Sing it over and over and over again until the yearning, the longing in your heart, transforms into the virtue of patient trust.

Patient trust is the only way you or I will get through this complex life, as the fulfillments of many of our heart-held desires are delayed until the Bright Day a New Creation – when all our longings, spoken and unspoken – are fulfilled in the Person and Presence of Jesus.

REFLECTION

Are you good at waiting on the Lord? What songs help you in hard moments?

PRAYER

Spirit of God, I want to learn the virtue of patience from You, the Master of Waiting. I yield my will to You, and choose to trust You with every unfulfilled desire of my heart. You are the Keeper of Dreams, the Bottler of Tears, and the Rememberer of Promises. I wait patiently for You, Lord.

In Jesus' faithful Name,

Amen. +

19. DID YOU PRACTICE TODAY?

But Jesus often withdrew to lonely places and prayed.
Luke 5:16 (NIV)

Every musician knows how important practice is to becoming able, good, and eventually great at one's instrument. But most musicians I know struggle with consistency – with desiring to do what they actually have to do to achieve the dreams they've rehearsed in their heart.

When I first became a drummer in high school, I had one summer to learn how to play the triple toms (called trips) for my school's marching band. They were desperate; we were a competitive band in our state with a killer drumline led by an intense drum corp snare master.

But they had a gap, and I was eager to fill it – mainly because I was lonely sitting in the stands every Friday night, and most of my friends were in the band that was either on the field or pumping out music in their own stadium section.

The older student assigned to train me, who was an award-winning young drummer in our state, made the plan clear on the first day we met.

"Dan," he said with intensity in his voice, "This only works one way. You have to practice these same parts multiple times a day, every single day until the first full band practice. The parts have to become a part of you, and rehearsing them has to become as ordinary as breathing."

We met 3 times per week, every week of that summer, and he taught me how to practice – effectively, consistently, and with no wiggle room for my moods to dictate when or how I did so. I sacrificed much that summer to master my newly forming skill – and the stick tricks that were a part of the show.

I recorded my mentor playing the parts on a cassette tape, then made a new tape that repeated the parts for 90 minutes, one after the other. I fell asleep to that tape every night to get the sound of the parts in my head.

I was breathing the music by summer's end, and my parts were unforgettable. I had moved from hoping I wouldn't make a mistake to not being physically able to make a mistake.

After decades of being a Christian, I have come to believe that spiritual practices – daily rhythms through which we hone our ability to hear God's voice, train ourselves to be grateful, pray for what concerns us, and look with hope toward the hours ahead – are more crucial than I ever realized. In fact, they are literally life or death to a Christian's journey.

For me, my central spiritual practice – one which I do 8-9 times a day for at least 5 minutes – is the Daily Examen. It has become like breathing to me, and I now can't imagine waking or falling asleep without its pattern running through my head and heart.

Name your spiritual practices today that bring you to this moment. You are becoming what you do or do not do. Make sure your practices are holistic enough to cover all you need each day to stay strong in Jesus. The winds will come, and the crosses will appear. But like Jesus and His lonely place rhythms, your practices will have formed you for those moments.

REFLECTION

What practices do you currently do that help you walk intimately with Jesus each day? What new practices are you considering trying?

PRAYER

Spirit of God, there is often trouble in my soul because I have not gone into the training it takes to become the spiritual athlete the Apostle Paul encouraged me to become. Show me the rhythms I can begin to implement that You intend to use across my lifetime. And give me the will to practice my practices until they are as normal as breathing for me.

In Jesus' coaching, training Name,

Amen. +

20. WHAT'S ON YOUR BUSINESS CARD?

And a voice from heaven said, "This is my Son, whom I love; with him I am well pleased."
Matt. 3:17 (NIV)

Jesus is under the water, and the strong hands of John the Baptist are around His frame. Buried in the sea, this moment with Jesus foreshadows the tomb that will soon attempt to hold Him forever, after His life has been spent on a cross of hideous design.

The waters of the seas and the oceans, for the ancient Jews, represented *chaos* – the great unknown, the always-dangerous, and the spiritually-ominous. The sea represented the mysterious home of unimaginable creatures (remember Leviathan?) and the burial ground of mighty ships and their brave inhabitants.

Jesus enters these waters of chaos, represented by the Jordan River, then rose from their depths in the powerful image of baptismal resurrection. He was show-and-telling the rebirth of Israel in that moment, a people lost in spiritual chaos now being brought into the Father's holy order.

He was also showing us what would happen in our baptism as we died and rose with Christ, imaged by the immersion of our bodies into water and the raising of them up by a strength not our own.

And at Jesus' baptism, it happens. Jesus gets the only business card He will ever need at this moment of His world-bending beginning of ministry.

We hear from heaven:

"This is my Son, whom I love; with him I am well pleased."

Jesus has done nothing yet. No impressive miracles. No profound sermons delivered. No storied acts of justice. And from this place of utter non-performance, the Father has only one title to put under Jesus' name on his business card: *Son.*

First, the Father secures Jesus' identity – "This is my Son." Jesus, nothing will change that you are my boy. Nothing. Remember this.

Second, the Father expresses affection – "...whom I love." Jesus, I adore you. Before you face what you will face, I just want you to know how much I treasure you, how deeply I love you. You are my favorite, and my arms are around you.

Third, the Father empowers Him with affirmation – "...with him I am well pleased." Jesus, I'm already pleased with you before you do anything. You can't earn my love, and you will never need to; I love you now as much as I ever will.

With these few words, the Father launches Jesus into a ministry that will have Him speaking before eager crowds without a desire to court their favor (the battle with success), and dragging a cruel cross to His own execution without a need to resist (the battle with suffering).

The Father knew that Love – encircling Jesus within and without – would form the only armor He would ever need to see His mission through.

And so it is with us. Beneath your name, on your business card, belongs only one of two words: "Son" or "Daughter."

Your identity, like Jesus, is settled with the clear word of your child-status in your Father's heart. There is no performance, no role, no activity, no brokenness nor beauty in you that will ever take that away.

Remain in love, rooted and established in love, defined by love. And keep any stage, role, or action off your spiritual business card.

Just your name, and your identity as a son or daughter, is all you'll ever need.

REFLECTION

If you had to read your spiritual business card right now, what would it say? What has Jesus written there, and what have you added yourself?

PRAYER

Spirit of God, Your love is enough for me. Forgive me for asking a role, a title, a noble action, or a stage to love me or to sustain my identity. Only You can love me, secure me, and send me into today with the resources I need to face success or suffering. Rewrite my business card with me, that I may be affirmed by, motivated by, and led by Your Love – in all I do.

In Jesus' loving, leading Name,

Amen. +

21. THE MORNING GOD NEWS

Do you not know? Have you not heard? The Lord is the everlasting God, the Creator of the ends of the earth. He will not grow tired or weary, and his understanding no one can fathom.
Isaiah 40:28 (NIV)

The daily news cycle is always spinning, whirling, swirling, every day, telling us what is "new" and what we need to know if we are to lead a good life.

We are informed of the state of this war or that war, this failure or that failure, this injustice or that injustice. Then we are informed of the reactions to each bit of news being reported, giving us new insight on new happenings every new day.

Being up on the latest news, we are told, will keep us aware, healthy, activated, and safe. But knowledge can also be a burden, and knowing what is happening everywhere at all times can weigh us down – especially if we're not sure what new information is true or accurate.

God's News cycle is also always in motion. It runs 24 hours a day, just like the daily news cycle. It also is carefully selected, just like the daily news cycle. And worship is the soundtrack to God's News, God's Good News, God's True News. God's News comes to us from a perspective that knows every detail of your life and mine, as well as every detail of our past and every detail of our future.

For that reason, it may seem that God's News cycle is not committed to the news always being, well, "new." Some things, God knows, are very old – and we need to hear them again and again and again.

"Do you not know? Have you not heard?" is a great way to start this morning's God News. In fact, it's a great opening to a time of worship.

First, “do you not know” that your God is everlasting? Your Father is always alive, always awake to you, and always, always loving you.

Your Creator knows the times and seasons in your life and what brings you joy and pain. He is at work to help you, support you, teach you, train you, and to involve you in a far grander Story than the one you are most aware of right now.

Second, “have you not heard” that your God does not get tired, that your God does not find you frustrating or tedious or irritating or slow to get it? Have you not heard that God understands all that is going on in your life today and in the life of the planet, and is present to guide you, by the Spirit, into ways of thinking and feeling and acting that strengthen you and everyone around you?

Welcome to this morning's God News – the news that you, and everyone you will meet, are made by, and loved by, the Everlasting Creator today. Let the worship you lead resonate with the True, Right, Good, and Lovely God News today.

REFLECTION

What news are you most believing today?

PRAYER

Spirit of God, all of Your news is good news. I want to be aware of Your daily announcements, be on Your email list, be part of Your text thread. I want to hear, again and again, the words that bring me life, and that bring life to those around me. I want to listen closely to Your Word and stay close to Your heart. I am listening to Your news today.

In Jesus' pure, good, love-announcing Name,

Amen. +

22. THE FOUR LIVES WE LIVE

They devoted themselves to the apostles' teaching and to fellowship, to the breaking of bread and to prayer. Everyone was filled with awe at the many wonders and signs performed by the apostles. All the believers were together and had everything in common. They sold property and possessions to give to anyone who had need. Every day they continued to meet together in the temple courts. They broke bread in their homes and ate together with glad and sincere hearts, praising God and enjoying the favor of all the people. And the Lord added to their number daily those who were being saved....
Acts 2:42-47 (NIV)

I remember the first time I saw the text acronym "YOLO." Like most of these little textual wonders, I tried to cover my ignorance by figuring it out on my own before asking the person who sent it what it meant.

I'm sure I came up with at least 10 ideas, all of which were nonsensical. Then, I asked my son, who is always up on the latest text-speak. "Dad (he said with that implicit tone of 'you're so behind, old dude'), it means 'You Only Live Once.'"

Of course! YOLO! (I'm sure cats text each other YOLNT – You Only Live Nine Times – just to mock us.)

Our faith vision of eternity says that while we may only live once, life is forever – and there is a transition that takes place at death. But we also use language that recognizes we live more than just one life at a time – we actually have a few lives running side by side, like a symphony with many instruments.

"Don't let your work life overtake your personal life," we say, or "Make sure you care for your secret life with God." Your life, my life, is a symphony – and a variety of harmonies are meant to run alongside Christ's melody for a full and rich life to emerge.

The early Church, in the passage above, was following Jesus' model of life together. Scholars suggest there are four "lives" the Church was living post-resurrection in those early days, and I made up my own terms to help us remember them and reclaim them for ourselves.

First, the *Learning Life*. With the Scriptures (the teaching of the Apostles in this passage) at the center of our solar system, we are in a long learning of how to love, how to give, how to serve, and how to be human in the world. Be a lifelong learner.

Second, the *Sharing Life*. Fellowship is intended to be more than spiritual friendship, but not less. If we're not always sharing a common purse of money, land, or cars, we are at the very least to share our possessions in the tone and spirit of hospitality and wild generosity.

Third, the *Abounding Life*. Multiple times in this passage, the community of Christ is said to be breaking bread, meaning they were eating together with laughter and relational care (my translation of glad and sincere hearts). The Agape Feast was a time for enjoying one another, but also for remembering the mystery of Faith – Christ has died, Christ is risen, Christ will come again! And because they abounded in joy and vitality, they were a magnet to people who had never seen such love.

Fourth, the *Prayerful Life*. These "heaven-and-earth people" (N.T. Wright) understood that God's two spheres of reality had come together in Christ, and heaven-and-earth people recognize that God is listening, and acting, in a great loving overflow of ongoing conversation with each one of us.

I.e. It's not prayer that works; it is God who works in fresh ways when we pray, as He accesses our hearts and partners with us in spiritual influence as we do.

Imagine the world without these four threads of life running together! Many people don't just imagine it – they live in the pain of its lack every day. Let these four lives rise to the surface again in your life, and welcome the Lord to make you and your community a magnet for those craving such love.

REFLECTION

Of the four lives mentioned, in which do you feel the strongest? In which do you feel the weakest?

PRAYER

Spirit of God, Your life at work in us is what enables us to live a learning life, a sharing life, an abounding life, and a prayerful life with power and hope. Fill us again with renewed vision for the life You have always intended for us, Your people.

In Jesus' family-building, love-compounding Name,

Amen. +

23. HE WILL ACCOMPLISH WHAT CONCERNS YOU

The Lord will accomplish what concerns me; Your lovingkindness, O Lord, is everlasting; Do not forsake the works of Your hands.
Psalm 138:8 (NIV)

If your life is anything like mine, right now you're in the middle of a challenge. Our challenges may be different, and of different scales and sizes, but they are challenges nonetheless.

Each challenge tests our faith. It really does. Whether we're aware of it or not, we are inwardly believing in an invisible God – sometimes despite a brooding sense that He's being slow-on-the-draw to answer us, or somewhat stingy in His response, or not quite on top of the things that concern us.

In some cases, your challenge may feel (or perhaps, be) relationship-threatening, vocation-threatening, or even life-threatening.

But there is the greater reality that supersedes the reality we are currently perceiving, and sometimes – if not most times – we have to sing it to get it into our bones.

Ready? Here it is. (Feel free to sing the following, to your own tune, instead of just reading it.)

God is good. God loves you. God is in this with you. You are not alone. He will accomplish what concerns you in the long run. He will also do this with the others involved. He will reveal His love to you. He will send you helpers along the way. He will expose broken areas in your life, and will simultaneously provide you with healing opportunities for you to become more like Him in your transformation. God is near. God is close. God is aware. God is present to your need, and acting even as we speak. Be attentive, be aware of what the Spirit is doing right now.

Because of God's seeming slowness to act, many people slowly lose faith over time, and some eventually lose their faith after a long, slow bleed. But for those who have locked in, who have not broken with the "hand that raises" them (George Herbert), the long, slow work of God is revealed over the many years of a lifetime.

Hang in there. Sing what is true, what is right, and what the Scriptures say is true of you, others, and the world. That's why we have them. Let that song lead you, and the Spirit fill you as you sing with all you've got from here into eternity.

And from that place of infilling, sing and play your heart out as you lead others into that same kind of long-haul, singing faith.

God will accomplish what concerns you.

REFLECTION

Is your heart in a state of encouragement or discouragement today? Can you bring it to Jesus right now, and welcome Him to speak into the deep places of your spirit?

PRAYER

Spirit of God, I'm not always as strong as I think I will be, or as I hope I will be, when challenges come my way. Fill me with the will to sing even if my will to pray is waning. As I pray in song, let the words I sing and professions of faith I make become truer than the thoughts I am believing about my situation. You love me. You're with me. And we're in this together.

In Jesus' endlessly comforting Name,

Amen. +

24. THE FRUIT IS REAL

But what happens when we live God's way? He brings gifts into our lives, much the same way that fruit appears in an orchard—things like affection for others, exuberance about life, serenity. We develop a willingness to stick with things, a sense of compassion in the heart, and a conviction that a basic holiness permeates things and people. We find ourselves involved in loyal commitments, not needing to force our way in life, able to marshal and direct our energies wisely. Galatians 5:22-23 (*The Message*)

A worship team is a community – a tribe – within a community. And that community is, in so many ways, a garden where Jesus walks.

We are first a community of disciples of Jesus who have said yes to the long, hard work of becoming like Christ by partnering with the Holy Spirit in the formation of our hearts and lives.

There is nothing that Jesus does not have access to in the garden of our hearts. Our attitudes, our emotions, our choices, our relationships, our gifts, and our skills – Jesus is Lord of all of it, or He is Lord of none of it.

We are secondly a community of creative and technical people, putting our energies toward serving our local church family in worship with the skills and abilities we have developed over a lifetime.

We serve one another in our roles, and we make sure that what we do is not for our own visibility or platform, but to honor Jesus and one another with humility, grace, and a willingness to lay down our opinions for a greater good.

In Galatians 5, the kinds of fruits that should be growing in our individual gardens, and in the garden of our worship team's heart, are clear. The Spirit is at work to make us loving (care for one another), joyful (laugh in light of our hope), peaceful (keep things clear between yourself and others), patient (others are worth waiting for), kind (let your words land softly on the souls of others), good (affirm the good in others at all times), faithful (be steady in your commitments), gentle (let tenderness lead), and self-controlled (watch your ways and guard your heart).

The community of our worship team can only be a garden for these kinds of fruit to grow if each one of us is committed to seeing ourselves as a garden where Jesus has full access to every part of our past, present, and future.

Today, make the choice to be a garden, and to be a garden together, where Jesus can make His orchard fruitful.

REFLECTION

What is the state of your personal orchard of the fruits of the Spirit? What part of the orchard needs the most attention right now?

PRAYER

Spirit of God, make us fruitful in love, joy, peace, patience, kindness, goodness, faithfulness, gentleness, and self-control today as a worship community. We choose Your life, growing in us, and growing as we work together to create beautiful spaces for our whole community to worship.

In Jesus' caring, tending Name,

Amen. +

25. THE GREAT EASTER GRAVE ROBBERY

Wake up from your sleep, climb out of your coffins; Christ will show you the light!
Ephesians 5:14b (*The Message*)

You can feel it in the wind, if you stand still in its movement. You can read it in the skies, if you're looking and longing to see writing eternal.

There is a Day coming that will leave us tearless, but for tears of joy. There is a Day coming that will leave us speechless, but for the Speech of the Ages.

It will be a Day of Theft. Of Robbery. Of Stealing. Of complete and utter Disappearance. And you and I will be accomplices of the best kind. It is the Day when our mortal and immortal Enemy – Death – will be left bereft of power, of strength, of life, or hold, or grip, or grasp, or meaning, or treasure, or name.

Even memory of what it was, or might be, will simply pass away.

On that Day, Death will have its final sentence read aloud for all the universe to hear. The pronouncement will be made, and the long travail will be over. Death will be sentenced to death, and will cease to exist – to be forgotten forever.

However we read the Jesus story, it whispers, it shouts, it sings of a Day – a set moment and season that will open in time – when a dying Death will breathe its very last.

And it's already in motion.

If not for the Easter intervention, the spiritual death for which you and I were destined, would be our natural end.

Name it what you will – a life of fear, of compulsion, of entitlement, of hatred or desperation or quiet, self-absorbed lifestyle contentment – the cold hand of Death is always laying a trail of crumbs to lead us to itself.

And the Death of the body always follows the death of the heart. We are all breathing our last breaths, fighting our last fights, and singing our last songs in this body as we know it.

Enter Easter – the Great Grave Robbery. The heart knows faith instead of fear. The heart is compelled by love, rather than by loose affections, money, achievement, or despair.

And the body? Your grave will be empty. So will mine. So, as you love, as you lead, and as you worship this Always-Easter season, feel the narrative changing.

Cease to see Death as the mover of the plot.

See Jesus, the Great Life-Eternal Protagonist, robbing Death blind at every turn toward the final, faithful, ferocious plundering of Darkness on All-Things-Are-Made-New Day.

REFLECTION

How does worship, in your church, affirm the resurrection life in your community week after week? What part do you play?

PRAYER

Spirit of Life, this is Your Season. I embrace the Life gifted to me, and given to me to give to others. I take my place as Your accomplice in the most Sacred Theft in history. Train me to steal Death's holdings as I follow You in Your great work of loving the world to life. And as I do, continue the deep, New Creation work You have begun in me.

In Jesus' resurrection-bringing Name,

Amen. +

26. SAY YES AND NO TO YOURSELF

Next Jesus was taken into the wild by the Spirit for the Test. The Devil was ready to give it. Jesus prepared for the Test by fasting forty days and forty nights.
Matthew 4:1-2a (*The Message*)

How do you feel when you hear these words? *Passion, freedom, give, receive, full, generous, lavish, enjoyment, pleasure, delight, go?*

Now, how do you feel when you hear these words? *Restraint, limitation, withhold, resistance, empty, scarcity, abstinence, displeasure, pain, stop?*

Most of us, unlike other generations, respond far more positively to the first set of words, and far more negatively to the second. Like it or not, we swim in a culture of pleasure, and, in our view, God would only care about, or be characterized by, words that speak of generosity and giving and enjoyment.

We are indeed a generation that needs to know and receive the fullness of the lavish love and the border-breaking permissions of God. But, we are also a generation that is chained by both public and secret lack of restraint, self-control, and multiple levels of addiction via the dopamine hit that is pleasure.

We should remember something Jesus taught us in the desert: The Destroyer knows exactly how to tempt – how to test the limits – of someone who is good at saying "Yes" to themselves, and "Yes" to others.

But what the Destroyer fears most is someone who has also learned to say "No" to themselves, and even to others, along the way.

Jesus prepares for his wilderness battle not by strengthening himself with food and drink and community and laughter and joy, but by intentionally entering into a 40-day season of saying "No" to his appetites, desires, enjoyments, and delights.

It was not Jesus' indulgence that prepared him for the confrontation of his life; it was his *abstinence*.

His capacity to say no to himself was fortified by the love He experienced in His baptism just a short time before, and by implementing the abstaining habits and practices that were integral to His very Jewish faith.

Saying "No" to oneself through law-keeping, fasting, praying, isolation, and other patterns and practices of self-restraint fortified Him and enlarged His capacity to reign in His passions when invited to delights that would ultimately derail His purpose and deform the truly human being He was, and is, and will always be.

Practice saying "No" to yourself for seasons: to food, to drink, to spending, to getting, to physical pleasure, to your passions, or to your own will being done in order to prepare yourself better to battle the Destroyer who is, at this very moment, after your life.

With Jesus as our model, walk into the wild with both the Yes of Passion and the No of Restraint as your spiritual weapons in the war for your soul.

REFLECTION

Is there anything you need to say "Yes" to right now, and anything you need to say "No" to at the same time?

PRAYER

Spirit of God, I do love the joys and freedoms You give to us in life. And I want to enjoy all You have given, without letting my armor become soft by always saying "Yes" to myself. I embrace the passions You have put in me, as well as the restraints through which You will train me. Teach me, as You did in the desert, to say "No" to myself that I may thrive for Your glory, and my health.

In Jesus' generous, lavish, abstaining, spirit-training Name,

Amen. +

27. ENJOY YOUR LIFE

You make known to me the path of life; in your presence there is fullness of joy; at your right hand are pleasures forevermore.
Psalm 16:11 (NIV)

My grandfather, as he was dying of heart disease in his 60s, would sit on his front porch with me on a swing, his oxygen mask on and his little cup of ice chips in hand (all the liquid he was allowed to have). We would slowly swing back and forth together while he poured his wisdom into my teenage heart.

He would talk to me about girls, about work, and about what it means to have a fulfilled life. At one point he said to me, "Dan, I want you to never forget this: Joy is not something that happens to you; true Joy is found in knowing a Person."

Early in the morning on the day my grandfather died, I was sitting with him at his bedside. He was gripping my hand and, in his delirium, he was calling out for old Army buddies, for his mommy, and for others that came to his unfiltered mind.

Then, suddenly, he stopped.

He grabbed my hand with as much strength as he'd had when he was healthy, and he looked me deep in the eye. "Daniel!" he said with steel in his voice, "Enjoy your life! Jesus will take care of you. I love you, I love you, I love you...." His voice trailed off as he slipped back into his delirium.

I was stunned. As my eyes welled up with tears there at his bedside, I recognized that my grandfather had left me a legacy in his final moments.

When he said, "Enjoy your life," I now know what he meant. He meant for me to place the One who is Joy at the center of my bright days and dark nights, and to revel in the family and friends that He would give me along my journey.

My grandfather passed through the veil that day – with his arms raised to heaven in the ambulance, saying, "Jesus, I see You; I'm coming...." For him, his Joy was now complete.

I have never forgotten that day. Nor have I forgotten that Joy – true Joy – is found in knowing a Person. Joy is meant to be experienced daily by constant attention to this priority relationship in our lives.

We allow Christ's Joy to indwell and encourage us along this journey. That is what it means to enjoy life. As a worshipper, I encourage you – pursue the Person who is Joy.

REFLECTION

How are you currently experiencing Joy in your life? Do you sense the Lord is behind it?

PRAYER

Spirit of God, there is a confidence that marks a life that knows what it means to be near You. As we grow in an intimate friendship with You, our designs to achieve and succeed begin to diminish, and we begin to desire to know You as we are known by You. I take hold of Your presence with me, and I will learn to walk this world's wild terrains with Joy at Your side. You are with me, and You are my source of Joy.

In Jesus' joy-making, life-sealing Name,

Amen. +

28. I BET I CAN MAKE YOU SMILE

The LORD your God is with you… He will take great delight in you; in his love he will… rejoice over you with singing."
Zeph. 3:17, selections (NIV)

When you woke up this morning, what was the first thought you had about yourself? First thoughts that come to us when we wake are usually some evaluation of how we feel, or something we need to do. "I feel tired; I shouldn't have stayed up so late," "I need to get a new pillow," or "How am I going to get everything done I need to do today?"

Then, perhaps your thoughts wander to yourself, and to the state of your life. You might be a saint who quickly moves to thanking God for the new day ahead of you, or you might be like the rest of us and think primarily about whether you actually like who you are or not.

Would it surprise you to know that, according to the Scriptures, God is present to you as you've been sleeping (Ps. 121:4)? That He's not only awake when you are awake? Your Father is ever-awake, ever-aware, and ever-watching you.

For some of us, that might make us nervous! But, let's step back and imagine what God might be thinking when we wake up.

I imagine the moment might be similar, every morning, to the moment a baby wakes up while a parent or grandparent is watching.

"There you are! Good morning, sweetheart. I love you. Did you sleep well? It's so good to see you; yes it is." Then, with a kiss on the forehead, and a warm hug, the day begins.

There is nothing to be fixed. Nothing to be corrected. Only love, affection, and delight in you.

Consider the possibility that the thoughts your loving Father is having about you as you wake to each new day are not about what needs to be fixed in you, what is wrong with you, what problem needs to be dealt with in your life, or which way He will use to teach you to have a little more faith (because you are just so darn slow to learn).

Consider that you are *always* delightful. You *always* make Him smile, and chuckle, and so glad that He made you to share life with Him. You are worth all of that affection in His overflowing, all-knowing heart. You are precious. You are valuable. You. Are. Fine.

Then, as the day begins, consider that God begins to say...

"Now, precious one, what can we get out of the way so that you can see yourself the way I see you? So you can like yourself, even love yourself, the way I love you? What is tangling you up, confusing you, making you afraid, or causing you to hurt others without realizing it? Let's touch those things so you can begin to enjoy the life that we have together, with those I've given you to share it with."

You are delightful to God. Jesus named you "Beautiful" before you ever combed your hair or put on your makeup. You are beloved. You are treasured. You are adored. And that is a reason, right now, to smile. Go ahead; no one but God is looking.

Smile.

REFLECTION

How does it make you feel when you think about the pure affection the Father has for you today?

PRAYER

Spirit of God, the smile on my face is my reminder that You absolutely adore me today. I'm so thankful that we're in this together, because life can be very, very hard at times. Help me see myself the way You see me, and in the next few moments of my day, when my mind turns toward all that needs to be fixed in me, remind me that the goal is just to free me to be who You made me to be, and to help me live a life that brings delight to me and to others through me.

In Jesus' smile-inspiring Name,

Amen. +

29. GOD IS THE ANXIETY-BREAKER

So do not fear, for I am with you; do not be dismayed, for I am your God. I will strengthen you and help you; I will uphold you with my righteous right hand.
Isaiah 41:10 (NIV)

Have you ever experienced the raw, debilitating power of anxiety? For many of us who have, the grip of a paralyzing fear, repeated, relentless, and mercilessly assaulting one's mind is, as a poet-friend puts it, like having a python squeeze you to death – while telling you it's your own fault!

As someone who has experienced bouts with anxiety many times in my own journey as a worshipper and follower of Jesus, I smell its faint scent lingering in the cultural air we are all breathing these days. Fear, riding an anxiety-driven train and fueled by others around us who are not committed to being a non-anxious presence online, at work, or even in our homes, can seemingly destabilize and neutralize even the best Christian's prayers for peace.

How do we ourselves break free from the ropes of anxiety, and access Christ's triumphing presence in the face of our own need for peace?

I believe there is a key offered in this little verse from Isaiah. While I've drawn on many aids in the battle with anxiety, I've never found another key that ultimately opens up the lock and leaves anxiety's tentacles dying on the ground.

"Fear not, I am with you," resonate the words of this passage. And the statements that follow only have power because that first phrase exists.

"Fear not, I am with you." Do not be dismayed. "Fear not, I am with you." I am your God. "Fear not, I am with you." I will strengthen you. "Fear not, I am with you." I will uphold you. "Fear not, I am with you."

In the middle of the night, when my anxieties have kept me awake and deliverance feels far away, the knowledge that "God is with me" is sometimes all that has kept me going.
In worship, we personally and corporately must sing the promise of God, "I am with you," without halting, without faltering, during seasons of cultural anxiety.

And in seasons of personal anxiety, while I am drawing on all of my spiritual habits, my family, friends, the prayers of the saints, and other tools that keep me strong – I relentlessly sing and say this phrase until I am set free in my heart. God is ultimately the Anxiety-Breaker we need. Fill your home, your car, and your life with music that reminds you of the truth of His presence and His peace.

REFLECTION

Have you struggled with anxiety recently? How has the music of worship helped you through that season?

PRAYER

Spirit of God, today the world around me is spinning a narrative that makes me anxious, and keeps me on the defensive – even with You and those I am given to care for.
I choose to remember that You are with me, and out of the overflow of that repeated, held-onto-truth, I will be loving and generous to those around me. Help me to be a non-anxious presence, walking closely with You, through troubling times.

In Jesus' fear-halting Name,

Amen. +

30. AS A FATHER LOVES HIS CHILDREN

For you know that we dealt with each of you as a father deals with his own children, encouraging, comforting and urging you to live lives worthy of God, who calls you into his kingdom and glory.
1 Thessalonians 2:11-12 (NIV)

There is a quality of tenderness to the heart of God that many of us, perhaps most of us, struggle to identify with. You may have recently seen a father holding a newborn, tenderly rubbing the infant's back, whispering to the child, or even quietly singing and rocking the little one. Have you ever imagined God could be that way with you?

We understand that God is good, God is faithful, God is loving, and God is strong. In our most difficult moments of suffering, we understand that God is present, that God is aware, and that God is mysterious in His ways.

Singing "God, You are tender," while it may sound right on every level, can give us a slight internal pause. What does it mean for the Father to "deal" with us, tenderly, as an Encourager, a Comforter, and a Caller (v. 12)?

What does it mean to communicate the tenderness of God as we lead worship?

As an Encourager, there is a quality of tenderness that is reflected in God seeing something in you that you struggle to see in yourself.

As an Encourager, God then calls you to become something that He knows you are and can be, even if you don't perceive you are or could become who He sees you to be. There is no chiding, cajoling, or even tone of sternness in God's encouragement – there is only tenderness and belief in you.

As a Comforter, there is the quality of tenderness that is reflected when God is present with us in our grieving, our sadness, and our fear.

As a Comforter, God approaches us with warmth, affection, kindness, and stability. When we are weak, whether we feel it or not, there is His presence with us. Somehow, by the gift of Grace, we find a way to become strong by drawing from His tender presence in our weakest moments.

As a Caller, there is the quality of tenderness that calls us by name, rather than by a title or role.

We can almost hear God whispering our name into our ear as a father whispers to an infant, calling us to become one with Him, to unify our will with His, and to triumph over our fear with reminders of our precious nick-names before Him – perhaps the name that is "written on a white stone" (Rev. 2:17).

Allow the Father to work tenderly with you, and then lead others from that place of quiet strength.

REFLECTION

How has the Father expressed tenderness to you as of late? How has that impacted your personal worship experience?

PRAYER

Father God, Your tender love for me can feel like an alien object, especially at times when I am weak or my life is feeling out of control. But I remember that my feelings have never been the indicator of Your true nature.

You remain loving, kind, and strong no matter what state of

mind or heart I am in. I welcome Your tender love today, and rely on You for Your fatherly encouragement, comfort, and calling of my name.

In Jesus' loving, tender Name,

Amen. +

MY REFLECTIONS & NOTES

MY REFLECTIONS & NOTES

MY REFLECTIONS & NOTES

MY REFLECTIONS & NOTES

MY REFLECTIONS & NOTES

MY REFLECTIONS & NOTES

MY REFLECTIONS & NOTES

MY REFLECTIONS & NOTES

CONCLUSION

Thanks for coming along on this journey into the Scriptures, and into the heart of worship.

I hope the words in these pages have encouraged you, strengthened you, and given you fresh food for thought on your journey of participating in worship and its leadership in your local church.

I can't emphasize enough that the role you play matters - lives are moved forward into Christlikeness in the context of worship every single week. Christ is being formed in them, as the Spirit works in yielded hearts - in and through worship.

And that is both a responsibility and a privilege.

I'd like to continue encouraging you in your worship journey, and send you resources, through my email list at

www.DanWilt.com

Sign up for the email newsletter, and I'll send you more devotionals, as well as downloads, resources, and studies, that I trust will help to establish you in love and give you vision for the part you play in worship.

A BLESSING FOR YOU AS A WORSHIP SERVANT

Now, I'd like to leave you with a blessing as you faithfully serve your community in, and through, worship.

"I pray that out of his glorious riches he may strengthen you with power through his Spirit in your inner being, so that Christ may dwell in your hearts through faith. And I pray that you, being rooted and established in love, may have power, together with all the Lord's holy people, to grasp how wide and long and

high and deep is the love of Christ, and to know this love that surpasses knowledge—that you may be filled to the measure of all the fullness of God."

Ephesians 3:16-19 (NIV)

Grace and Peace, toward the Awakening of hearts to Christ,

Dan +

To order more copies of this devotional, search for
Songs Are A Place We Go on Amazon.com.

To sign up for Dan's email list, go to:

www.DanWilt.com

Songs Are A Place We Go
By Dan Wilt

Made in the USA
Middletown, DE
15 January 2021